# LIFE IS BETER WITH WINGS

## FLY LIKE A DRAGONFLY

## INSPIRATIONAL COLORING BOOK

### TAMMY CORWIN

© 2024 by Tammy Corwin. All rights reserved.

*Words Matter Publishing*
*P.O. Box 1190*
*Decatur, Il 62525*
*www.wordsmatterpublishing.com*



*ISBN 13: 978-1-962467-38-4*

*Library of Congress Catalog Card Number: 2024942619*

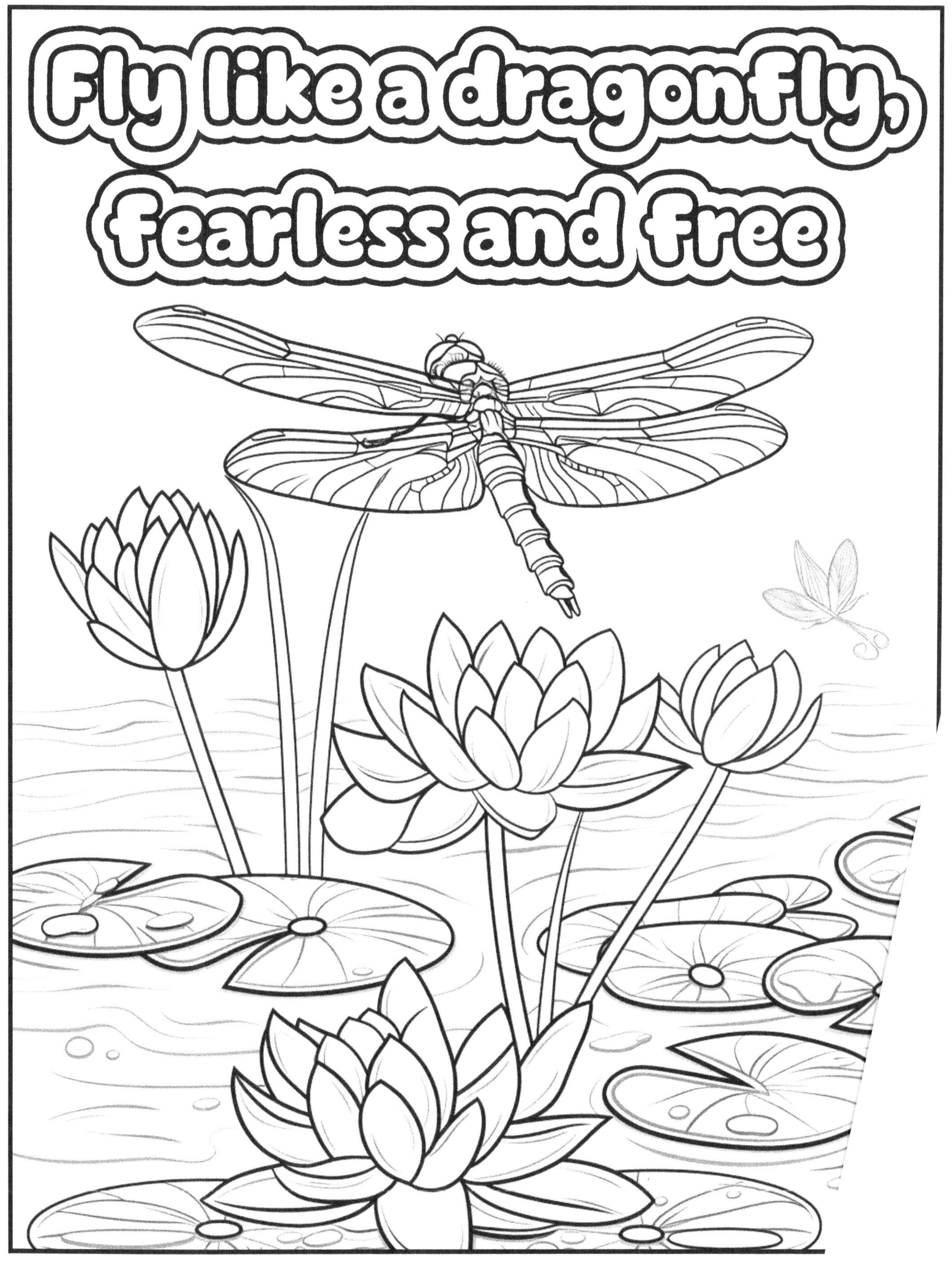

Fly like a dragonfly,
fearless and free

Glide Through Life With
The Elegance Of a Dragonfly

Dance on the wind,
resilient and bold

IN EVERY FLUTTER,
FIND YOUR
INNER STRENGTH

See life through the
multifaceted eyes
of a dragonfly

Rise above challenges
with dragonfly
grace

# STRENGTH IN EVERY BEAT

# OF YOUR WINGS

# Be a dragonfly:

## adapt, evolve, soar

Endure with elegance,
like a dragonfly

# IN THE FACE OF ADVERSITY,

# be a dRAGONFLY

Resilience is
BEAUTY IN MOTION

# FROM ADVERSITY, EMERGES STRENGTH AND LIGHT

LIFE'S TRIALS CAN'T
DIM A DRAGONFLY'S SHINE

Find your strength
in the dance
of the dragonfly

Embrace change
like a dragonfly

graceful like a
dragonfly,
fierce like
a warrior

Chase your dreams
with the spirit
of a dragonfly

Life is
better
with
DRAGONFLY
WINGS

Find your wings & fly like a dragonfly

Live light, travel light,
be a dRaGONFLY

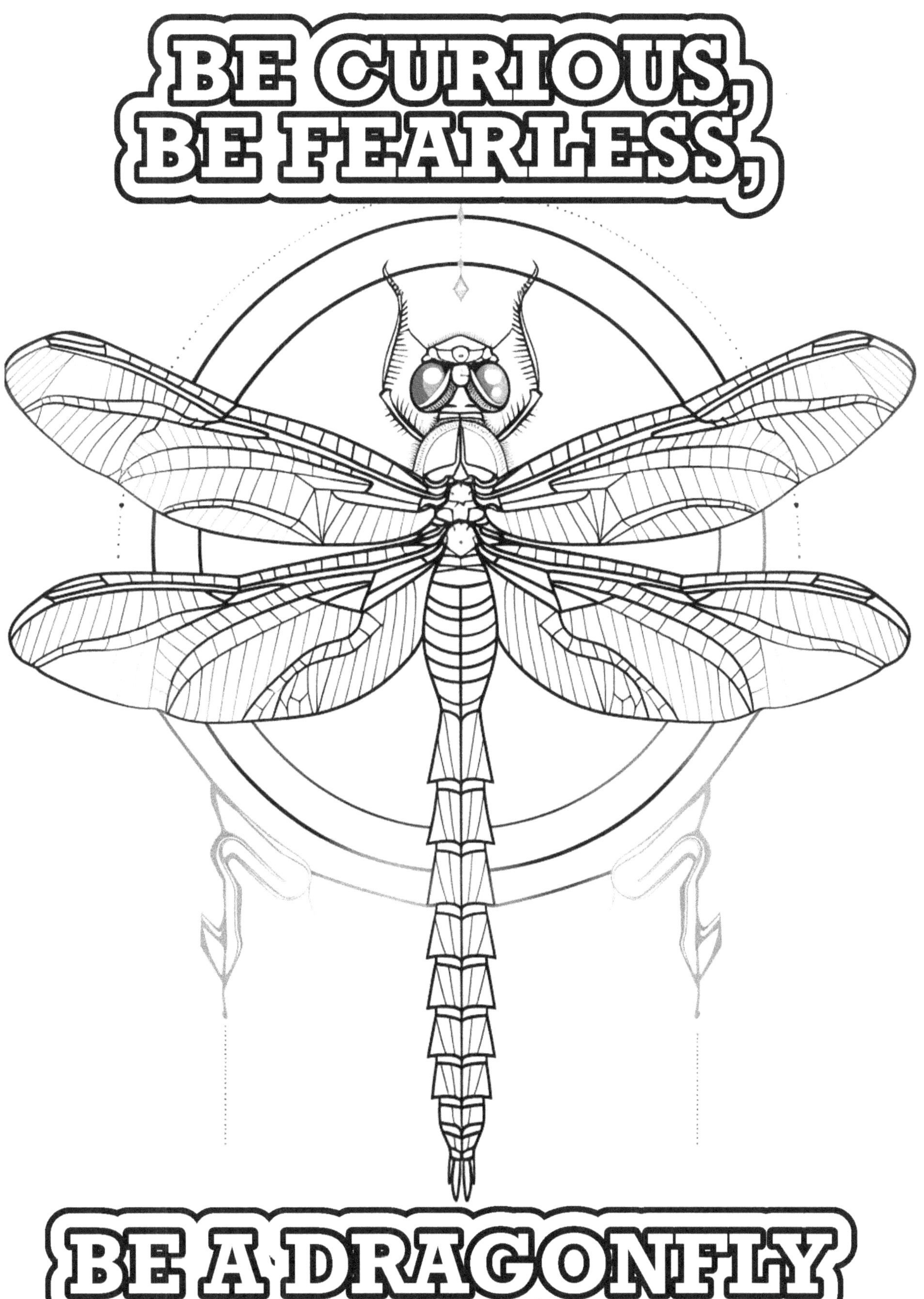

BE CURIOUS,
BE FEARLESS,
BE A DRAGONFLY

In a world full of flies,
be a dRaGONFLY

LIFE IS SHORT;
FLY HIGH LIKE
A DRAGONFLY

LET YOUR SPIRIT SOAR
LIKE A DRAGONFLY

Be a dragonfly
in a world of
mosquitoes

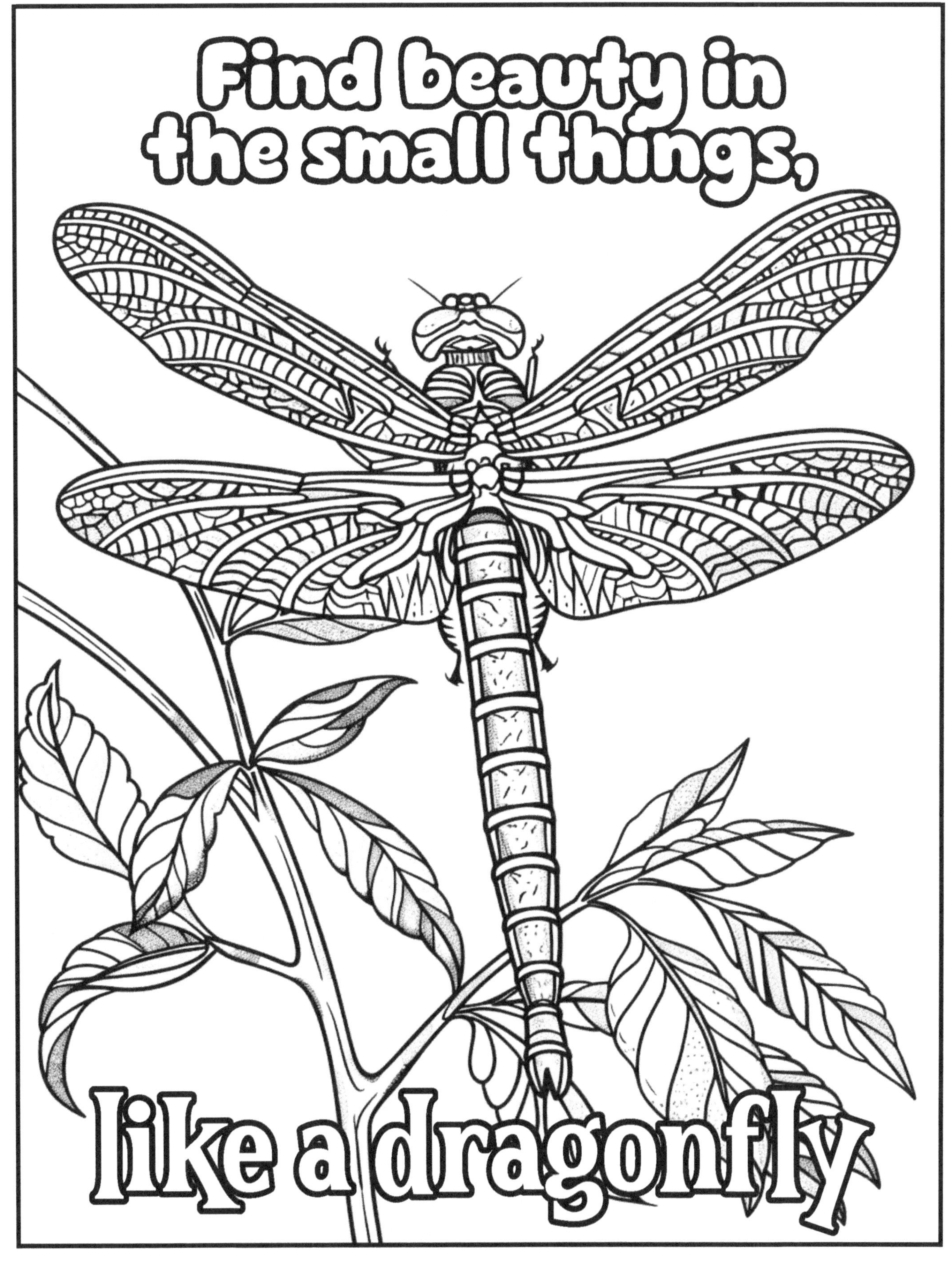

Find beauty in the small things,
like a dragonfly

Spread your wings
and fly like a dragonfly

TRANSFORM YOUR LIFE,
dRaGONFLY STYLE

In every dragonfly, there's a story of transformation

LIFE IS A JOURNEY;
MAKE IT A
DRAGONFLY ADVENTURE